THIS LAND CALLED AMERICA: COLORADO

CREATIVE EDUCATION

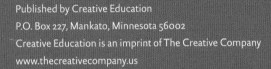

Published by Creative Education

P.O. Box 227, Mankato, Minnesota 56002

Creative Education is an imprint of The Creative Company

www.thecreativecompany.us

Book and cover design by Blue Design (www.bluedes.com)

Art direction by Rita Marshall

Printed in the United States of America

Photographs by Alamy (William Leaman, Visual Arts Library (London)),
Corbis (Bettmann, D. Robert & Lorri Franz, George H. H. Huey, Richard
Schabl/zeta), Getty Images (Laurance B. Aiuppy, Jess Alford, Alan
Band/Keystone Features, Paul Chesley, Willard Clay, David Clifford,
Dann Coffey, Daniel J. Cox, Tom Fowlks, Bill Heinsohn, Carl Iwasaki//
Time Life Pictures, John Kelly, Taylor S. Kennedy/National Geographic,
Charles Peterson/Hulton Archive, Karen Schulenburg, Harrison Shull,
James Thomas Thurlow/George Eastman House)

Library of Congress Cataloging-in-Publication Data

Peterson, Sheryl.

Colorado / by Sheryl Peterson.

p. cm. — (This land called America)

Includes bibliographical references and index.

ISBN 978-1-58341-631-0

1. Colorado—Juvenile literature. I. Title. II. Series.

F776.3.P48 2008.

978.8—dc22   2007005708

First Edition

9 8 7 6 5 4 3 2 1

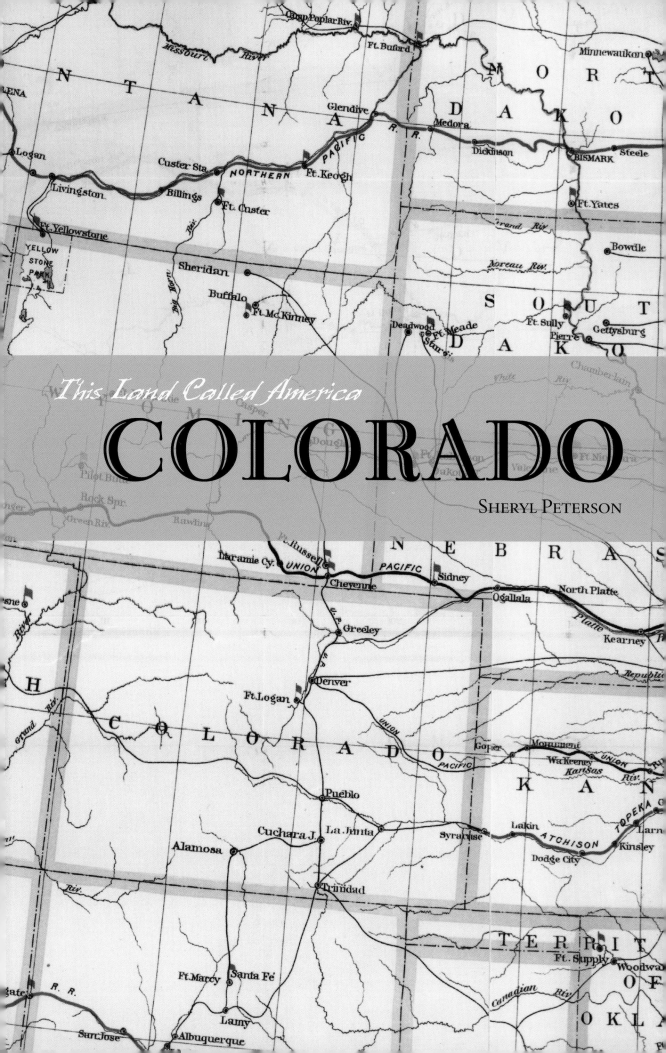

This Land Called America

COLORADO

Sheryl Peterson

Colorado

SHERYL PETERSON

EACH WINTER, AS THE SNOWFLAKES START TO SWIRL, COLORADO TURNS INTO A WHITE PLAY LAND. SKIERS AND SNOWBOARDERS COME FROM ALL OVER THE COUNTRY. THEY SPEND THEIR DAYS KNEE-DEEP IN FRESH, POWDERY SNOW. SKIERS ZIGZAG DOWN STEEP SLOPES AND GLIDE ALONG WELL-GROOMED TRAILS. NEXT, THEY HOP ON A CHAIRLIFT AND ENJOY A SCENIC RIDE. AT THE TOP, SOME PEOPLE REST AND GAZE AT THE BEAUTIFUL, SNOWCAPPED ROCKY MOUNTAINS. SOME GO INSIDE THE CHALET TO SIP A CUP OF STEAMY HOT CHOCOLATE. OTHERS CAN'T WAIT TO PUSH OFF AGAIN. THEY ARE READY TO ZIP OFF DOWN THE MOUNTAIN FOR ANOTHER COLORADO ADVENTURE.

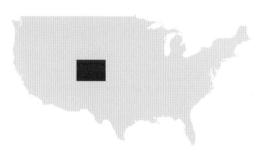

YEAR

1682 Explorer Robert de La Salle claims the area east of the Rocky Mountains for France.

EVENT

Westward, Wagons

HUNDREDS OF YEARS AGO, THE LAND OF COLORADO WAS A WILD AND BEAUTIFUL PLACE. ITS PURPLE MOUNTAINS AND GREEN VALLEYS CALLED TO EXPLORERS. MEN FROM SPAIN AND FRANCE TRAVELED WEST IN THE 1600S. THEY LOOKED OVER THE LAND AND CLAIMED IT FOR THEIR COUNTRIES. BUT THEY DID NOT STAY THERE.

Only the American Indians lived on the grasslands and hills of Colorado. The Cheyenne, Arapaho, and Ute Indian tribes hunted in the forests. They fished in clear Rocky Mountain streams. But in 1803, President Thomas Jefferson bought Colorado, along with the rest of the Louisiana Territory, from France.

Americans wanted to learn about the rugged new land. In 1806, Jefferson asked a young army officer to explore the wild country. His name was Zebulon Pike. After three long months, Pike's group of soldiers spotted a high peak. Pike climbed up through waist-deep snow. He was dressed only in cotton overalls and never reached the mountaintop. Even so, the peak was named Pikes Peak in his honor.

There were no towns in the far land, or frontier, of Colorado. In 1833, the first American post, called Bent's Old Fort, was built in the southeastern part of the state. The rustic fort was a fur-trading center and served as a rest stop for tired travelers.

When fur traders and explorers such as Kit Carson (above) were roaming the plains of the West during the 1800s, they encountered big herds of buffalo (opposite).

YEAR

1765 Spaniard Juan Maria Rivera explores the Rocky Mountains in search of gold.

EVENT

Early settlers who traveled west in covered wagons had to make their own paths through the wilderness.

Then, in 1858, prospector William Russell found gold in the Rockies. The news spread as fast as a wild prairie fire. People had "gold fever." They raced to western Colorado to pan for gold nuggets in the mountain streams. Many wrote "Pikes Peak or Bust" on their covered wagons. In the same year, Colorado's first army post, Fort Garland, was built. The leader of the fort was Kit Carson. Carson was a famous mountain scout and trapper.

More settlers came to Colorado's high plains in the last part of the 1800s. Under the Homestead Act of 1862, if farmers worked the land for five years, they could claim it as their own. These farmers were called "sodbusters." They built their houses out of sod, or pieces of ground, since there was not much wood on the plains.

Life was hard for sodbusters. Families planted wheat, corn, and sugar beets in the rich soil. But sometimes, huge clouds of grasshoppers landed on fields. The hungry insects stripped every wheat stalk bare.

In 1876, the United States turned 100 years old. That year, Colorado became a state. It was nicknamed the "Centennial State." Denver became the capital and an important supply center for the gold camps in the mountains. Denver's elevation was so high that it became known as "The Mile-High City."

Bent's Old Fort, near La Junta, Colorado, has been rebuilt out of adobe to look like it did in the 1840s.

The U.S. receives eastern Colorado from France as part of the Louisiana Purchase.

Some sod houses had normal doors and even windows, but the dirt structures were easily damaged.

More brave pioneers traveled west in the late 1800s. The huge herds of hairy buffalo that had once roamed the plains were almost gone by then. Many buffalo were killed just for sport and sometimes even shot at by train riders.

Colorado's American Indians were forced to move to the southwestern corner of the state. They lived in isolated villages called reservations. In 1880, an Indian chief named Ouray talked to the nation's leaders about keeping traditional Indian lands. But Chief Ouray's wish went ignored.

More Colorado land was opened up to settlers. By 1890, the state had two railroads. Trains linked Colorado to the rest of the nation. Many more people came from the East Coast to make Colorado their home.

People took burros up Pikes Peak in the 1800s, but today the summit can also be reached by car.

YEAR
1806
EVENT

Lieutenant Zebulon Pike and his soldiers discover Pikes Peak, a 14,110-foot (4,301 m) mountain crest.

- 10 -

Mountain State

THE WESTERN STATE OF COLORADO IS A RECTANGLE WITH SEVEN OTHER STATES ON ITS SIDES. IN THE SOUTHWEST, UTAH, ARIZONA, NEW MEXICO, AND COLORADO COME TOGETHER AT "FOUR CORNERS." IT IS THE ONLY SPOT IN THE U.S. WHERE FOUR STATES MEET. OKLAHOMA AND KANSAS TOUCH COLORADO'S EASTERN SIDE. NEBRASKA AND WYOMING ARE NEIGHBORS TO THE NORTH.

Colorado's diverse land area was formed by giant glaciers and volcanoes. The flat lands in eastern Colorado were once grasslands where millions of buffalo grazed. Now the land is dotted with farms, ranches, small towns, and cities.

A monument to the Four Corners is located in the middle of land owned by the Navajo Nation.

In the far west is the Colorado Plateau. This part of the state has deep valleys and steep, flat-topped hills. The hills are called mesas, which is Spanish for "tables." High, wide valleys, or "parks," lie between the mountain ranges. One of these parks is the San Luis Valley. It is the highest and largest mountain desert in North America. Natural hot springs bubble and steam in this area.

Colorado's mountains are its most recognizable feature. The Rocky Mountain range runs down the middle of the state. It looks like a spine of tall, snowcapped peaks. Colorado sits at a higher elevation than any other state. The tallest peak in the state is Mount Elbert, at 14,440 feet (4,401 m) above sea level.

At the base of the Sangre de Cristo mountains in Colorado's San Luis Valley lie the Great Sand Dunes.

The Continental Divide runs along the top of the Rockies. It is a line that marks the direction in which water flows. Rivers on the eastern side of the line flow to the Atlantic Ocean. Rivers on the western side flow to the Pacific Ocean.

YEAR
1848   Mexico gives western Colorado to the U.S. in the Treaty of Guadalupe Hidalgo.
EVENT

- 13 -

CONTINENTAL DIVIDE
LOVELAND PASS
ELEV. 11992 FT.

| ATLANTIC OCEAN WATERSHED | PACIFIC OCEAN WATERSHED |

T he weather in Colorado is mostly cool and dry. Colorado has more sunny days than most states in the U.S. Since Colorado receives a lot of snow, skiers often enjoy good mountain skiing from November through mid-May.

In December 2006, two giant blizzards piled several feet of snow on the state. Everyone was snowbound. More than 30,000 head of cattle were stranded. Ranchers had to drop hay from airplanes to feed the animals.

Gold made Colorado's mountains famous. But there are other rocks and minerals in the hills. Indians made sharp arrowheads from hard rocks such as chalcedony. They also used colorful turquoise stones in jewelry. Today, coal and shale help heat Colorado homes and fertilize farmers' fields.

A sign in the Rocky Mountains marks the location of the Continental Divide (above); a hiker climbs in the Rockies near American Basin (opposite).

Colorado fishermen can take advantage of the state's plentiful lakes and reservoirs year-round.

More rivers begin in Colorado than in any other place in America. The state has even been called "the mother of rivers." The Colorado River starts to flow in the western mountain slopes. It carries with it the red soil that gives the state its name. "Colorado" is a Spanish word that means "colored red." The Glen Canyon Dam was built on the river in 1963. The red soil is trapped behind the dam, and now the river water is a clear, blue-green color.

Colorado has more than 2,000 lakes. The mountain lakes were carved out of the rock by glaciers. The state's largest natural lake is Grand Lake. Not all of Colorado's lakes are natural, though. Some are man-made lakes called reservoirs.

Fishermen can fly-fish for trout or fish out of a boat for walleyes. Other people enjoy Colorado's lakes by clicking their cameras. Colorado always makes for a great picture.

YEAR

1858 Gold is discovered where the Cherry Creek flows into the Platte River near Denver.

EVENT

Gunnison National
Forest is named for John
William Gunnison, the
man who first explored
the area.

The fencing in of wild prairie land so that settlers could raise cattle (below) is partly what Chief Ouray (seated center, opposite) fought against.

Colorado becomes the second state in the U.S. to give voting rights to women.

Rocky Mountain Home

Many different American Indian tribes once lived in Colorado. The Cheyenne and Arapaho lived on the prairies. The Utes, or "Blue Sky People," loved life in the mountains. Soon, people came across the ocean from Europe, and families traveled from America's East Coast. They filled up the open spaces.

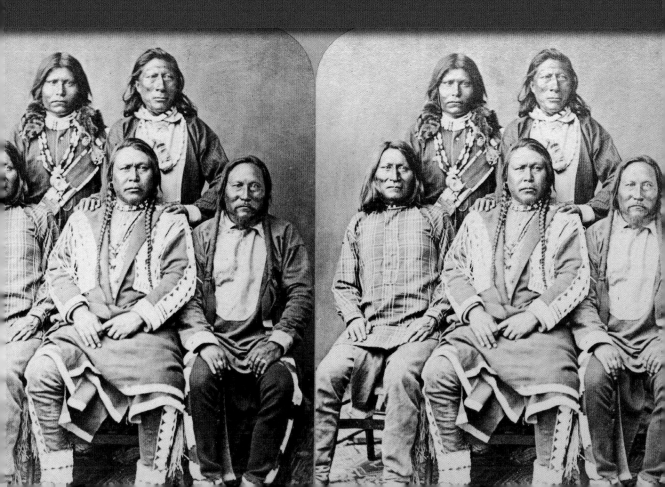

State bird: lark bunting

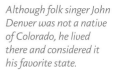
Some of Colorado's early settlers came to farm the land. Others wanted to get rich in the gold mines. In 1893, Katherine Lee Bates came for a vacation in the Rocky Mountains. Bates picnicked in the Pikes Peak area and gazed at the mountains around her. Then she started writing. Bates wrote a poem called "America the Beautiful." The poem was set to music. People loved the song. It became a big hit across the U.S.

Colorado is home to writers, artists, and musicians. People like to write, paint pictures, and sing about the mountains. The state's best-known singer was John Denver. He lived in Aspen for a time and wrote folk songs such as "Rocky Mountain High." That song became Colorado's second state song in 2007. Denver's real name was Henry John Deutschendorf Jr. He changed his last name to honor his adopted home state.

Another well-known Coloradan was Glenn Miller. Miller and his orchestra made "Big Band" music famous. Silent movie star Douglas Fairbanks was a Colorado actor. He played the hero in such movies as *Robin Hood* and *The Three Musketeers*.

Each year, people visit and decide to stay in Colorado and make it their home. Most of them choose to live in the strip of towns along the eastern side of the Rockies from Fort Collins to Pueblo. More than half of all Coloradans live in

YEAR

1913   "The Big Snow" of 1913 covers all of Colorado in three to five feet (.91–1.5 m) of snow.

EVENT

YEAR

1917   Wild West hero William "Buffalo Bill" Cody dies and is buried west of Denver.

EVENT

Trombonist Glenn Miller started his first band while attending high school in Fort Morgan.

Denver. Most are white. Spanish or Mexican people are the next largest group. African Americans and Asian Americans make up a smaller percentage.

Denver may have many tall buildings downtown, but it also has the largest city park system in the U.S.

The first jobs in Colorado were in the gold mines. Men dug the gold ore out of the hills. Then they traded the gold for supplies at the nearest general store. Nathaniel Hill was a Colorado senator who knew about mining. In 1868, he built the first large smelting machine to separate and melt the gold ore. Today, most mining in Colorado is done for coal instead.

Now people have many different jobs in Colorado. Farmers grow wheat, corn, and potatoes. Ranchers herd sheep and raise cattle. Some people work in the food industry, build roads, or work at one of Colorado's famous ski resorts. The state capital of Denver is a banking center. Denver is known as the "Wall Street of the West."

YEAR
1958   The U.S. Air Force Academy is built near Colorado Springs to train Air Force officers.
EVENT

Tourists love to visit Colorado. In the winter, visitors flock to resorts such as Aspen, Vail, and Keystone. They ski, shop, and eat at fine restaurants. In the other seasons, visitors hike the mountain trails. The adventurous ones raft down white-water rapids. And some tourists visit old ghost towns or soak in the hot springs.

People who live in Colorado get outside and lead healthy lives. Some studies say that Coloradans live longer than other Americans. Maybe this is because there are lots of places to exercise. Maybe it's the fresh mountain air, too. But there is less oxygen in the Colorado air, since the state is so high up. Visitors need to remember to drink lots of water and to rest often.

Mountain bikers (above) need to wear plenty of sunscreen when they are out on the trails; many people appreciate Colorado's bounty of national forests (opposite) and parks.

YEAR
1974   Denver allows African American and white children to attend the same schools for the first time.
EVENT

Colorado Cool

IN WINTER, SKIING IS KING IN SNOWY COLORADO.
STEAMBOAT SPRINGS IS A ONE-OF-A-KIND SKI TOWN.
RANCHERS STILL WALK THE STREETS IN THEIR OLD
COWBOY HATS AND BOOTS. BUT ON THE SLOPES, THERE IS
A NEW SKI LIFT. IT IS CALLED THE SUNSHINE EXPRESS. THE
LIFT SPEEDS UP THE MOUNTAIN AND IS POWERED ONLY BY
THE SUN AND THE WIND.

Hikers love to visit Pikes Peak. The peak is made of a pink-colored rock called granite. Zebulon Pike never made it to the top, but hundreds of other people have. Early visitors rode horses or mules up the mountain. Now people ride on the Pikes Peak Cog Railroad.

On a hill nearby is the oldest tree in the area. It is a Rocky Mountain bristlecone pine. The tree has been growing for about 2,040 years. Only six scientists know where the tree is located. The scientists keep it a secret as they study samples from the tree's inner core.

There is a special park in the valley below Pikes Peak called the Garden of the Gods. The park has tall, red sandstone shapes. Long ago, the Ute Indians thought that these rocks had once been giants. They believed that the Great Spirit had turned the giants into stone. Most likely, the rocks were formed by wind and rain. Some of the rocks have names such as Kissing Camels, Siamese Twins, and Toad and Toadstools. Railroad owner Charles Perkins gave the park to the state in 1909. He wanted it to always be free and open to the public.

Colorado's unique natural features include the Garden of the Gods (opposite) and bristlecone pines (above).

Broncos, known for their feistiness, lend their name to Colorado's National Football League team.

North of Colorado Springs is the U.S. Air Force Academy. It is one of the places where men and women train to be Air Force pilots and officers. On the outdoor grounds, a huge airplane is on display. Visitors may be able to watch pilots take off and land in U.S. Air Force Thunderbirds.

Most professional sports teams in Colorado are at home in Denver. The Denver Broncos play football in Mile High Stadium. In the 1980s, quarterback John Elway was a superstar for the Broncos. The team was called the "Orange Crush" because it wore orange jerseys. The Denver Nuggets are the state's pro basketball team. The state's hockey team is the Colorado Avalanche, and the Colorado Rockies play baseball.

With no shortage of snowy ski slopes and natural cliffs, Colorado offers skiers constant excitement.

YEAR
2000 Forest fires burn more than 44,000 acres (17,807 ha) in southwestern Colorado.
EVENT

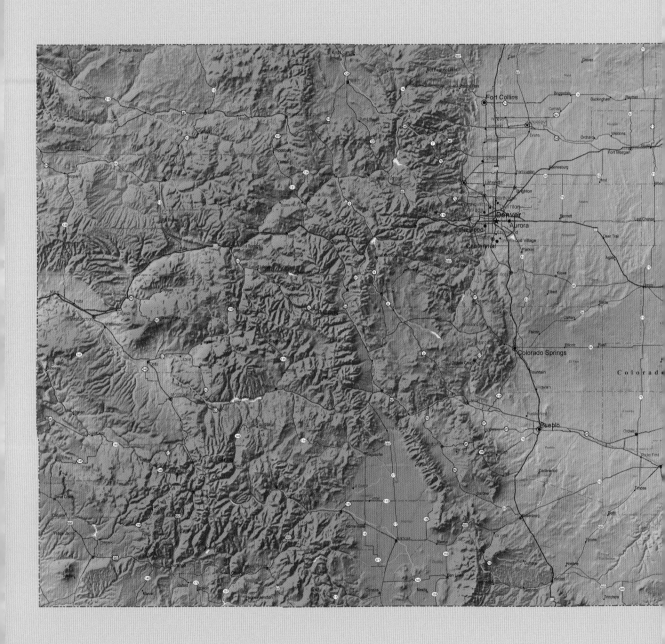

YEAR

2002   Governor Bill Owens is re-elected by the greatest majority vote in state history.

EVENT

- 30 -

QUICK FACTS

Population: 4,753,377

Largest city: Denver (pop. 557,478)

Capital: Denver

Entered the union: August 1, 1876

Nickname: Centennial State

State flower: Rocky Mountain columbine

State bird: lark bunting

Size: 104,094 sq mi (269,602 sq km)—8th-biggest in U.S.

Major industries: manufacturing, farming, mining, tourism

Rodeos are a part of Colorado western tradition. They date back to the 1880s. Bronco busting, bull roping, steer wrestling, and barrel racing are fun to watch. Rodeo fans today can visit the Pro Rodeo Hall of Champions in Colorado Springs.

When President Teddy Roosevelt once said that words alone could not describe Colorado, he was probably picturing Rocky Mountain National Park. The park has 17 mountains, thick pine forests, and numerous walking trails. Visitors may see wide-antlered moose and large herds of elk and bighorn sheep. They may also spy river otters sliding down the banks of the Colorado River or beavers gnawing on trees.

Colorado is a land of wonder to anyone who sees it. Visitors travel to hike the rugged mountain trails. Skiers can't wait to glide in the powdery snow. People who want a fresh start in a land with plenty of fresh air pack up and move to Colorado. And those who already live in Colorado marvel at the natural beauty of their home state every day.

YEAR
2007   Construction on America's largest solar energy plant begins in the San Luis Valley.
EVENT

- 31 -

BIBLIOGRAPHY

Caughey, Bruce, and Dean Winstanley. *The Updated Colorado Guide*. Golden, Colo.: Fulcrum Publishing, 2005.

Colorado Government Offices. "State Facts and History." State of Colorado. http://www.colorado.gov/colorado-government-links/state-facts-history.html.

Colorado State Tourism Office. "Kid's Page." Colorado State Tourism. http://www.colorado.com/magazine_section.php?id=7.

Frommer, Arthur, et al. *Frommer's USA 2000*. Hoboken, N.J.: Wiley Publishing, 2000.

Ginnodo, Bill , and Celia Ginnado. *Seven Perfect Days in Colorado*. Arlington Heights, Ill.: Pride Publications, 2002.

Klusmire, Jon. *Compass American Guides: Colorado*. New York: Compass American Guides/Fodor's, 1992.

INDEX

American Indians 7, 10, 14, 19, 27
  Chief Ouray 10
animals 10, 13, 14, 23, 31
Bates, Katherine Lee 20
Bent's Old Fort 7–8
border states 12
bristlecone pine trees 27
Carson, Kit 8
Colorado Springs 28, 31
Continental Divide 13
Denver 8, 23, 28
Denver, John 20
Fairbanks, Douglas 20
Garden of the Gods 27
gold rush and mines 8, 20, 23
Homestead Act 8
industries 8, 13, 23
  farming 8, 13, 23
  major businesses 23
land regions and features 5, 6, 7, 8, 13, 16, 19, 20, 24, 31

forests 7, 31
grasslands 7
highest point 13
hot springs 13, 24
lakes and rivers 13, 16, 31
mountains 5, 6, 7, 8, 13, 16, 19, 20, 24, 31
Louisiana Purchase 7
Miller, Glenn 20
natural resources 14, 23
Pike, Zebulon 7, 27
  Pikes Peak 7, 27
population 19, 20, 23
  countries represented 19
recreation 5, 14, 16, 24, 26, 31
sports 28
  professional teams 28
state nicknames 16
statehood 8
U.S. Air Force Academy 28
weather and climate 14